Frederick S. Daniel

Richmond Howitzers in the War

Four Years Campaigning with the ARMY of Northern Virginia

Frederick S. Daniel

Richmond Howitzers in the War
Four Years Campaigning with the ARMY of Northern Virginia

ISBN/EAN: 9783337814182

Printed in Europe, USA, Canada, Australia, Japan

Cover: Foto ©ninafisch / pixelio.de

More available books at **www.hansebooks.com**

RICHMOND HOWITZERS

IN THE WAR.

FOUR YEARS CAMPAIGNING WITH THE
ARMY OF NORTHERN VIRGINIA.

By a member of the Company.

RICHMOND:
1891.

RICHMOND HOWITZERS

IN THE WAR.

CHAPTER I.

In the month of April, thirty years ago, Richmond, living with methods and ways of long inheritance, possessing unequalled political influence and social importance, had a unique character. There was no other city like it in the United States; other cities enjoyed great material prosperity, but none of them approached Richmond's great qualities and high eminence. It was pre-eminently distinguished as a centre of genuine home and family life, which is the only basis of either provincial or national greatness. Its society, as the natural outcome of this condition, was most charming,

refined, and cultured. Its status was due to no purely artificial causes, no accidental institution, but mainly to superior and steady developments out of a strong race—the great English race that during two centuries had been transplanted to Virginia's soil and had been improving under favorable conditions. The early introduction and retention of negroes had primarily nothing to do with the making of Virginia, and was undoubtedly a serious drawback, a standing incubus in many ways on the community, save as it perhaps served to keep intact and compact the purity and strength of the great founding race. Fortunately the latter has now been developed into such powerful numbers—fifteen millions of homogeneous people in the South— that it needs no barrier or bulwark, excepting the most elementary rules of self-protection, for even continental Europe's millions could not swamp or crush out the now spreading growth from the old English nucleus.

Virginia has been prolific; for out of her limits have gone forth settlers into the immense Southland and into every part of the Union, and to-day, after all her vicissitudes, numbers 1,014,680 white citizens.

The Richmond of that day differed considerably from the Richmond of to-day. Naturally it has grown with added years, but special causes, or those resulting from the war, were chiefly instrumental in hastening its growth, nearly doubled in point of population, size, business, and embellishment. However, in 1861, Richmond was beautiful and measurably prosperous. The buildings, tasty and comfortable, were so many landmarks in the city, which was not behind in the conveniences and appliances of the period. It was much frequented by visitors, had many noted hotels and newspapers, stores well supplied, and a perennial source of profit in the State's favored staple products. The Legislatures that sat in the Capitol were not dwarfed by

the least usurpation on the part of the federal government, because Virginia was the leader of the Union, as she had been since the time of General Washington, or for over seventy years. Business, like the corporate limits themselves, was comparatively small, but yielded a comfortable support, without any splurging extravagance.

But, in April, 1861, to the charming quiet life that Richmond had so long been leading, a sudden standstill was put. An unexpected crisis confronted the city in a twinkling, and called for instant decision. Throughout the preceding winter the most animated discussions in regard to the secession of the South from the Union had been held in the Capitol, the press, the streets, and the homes; the political condition was extremely threatening, but Richmond did not want to see the Union broken; did all it could to prevent the occurrence, and sincerely cherished the hope that it would not be—that the clouds would roll by, the storm not burst. This hope, illusive

in reality, was held to amidst all the sharp, bitter contentions at home, despite all the insulting menaces and mockeries hurled across the border by the enemy that was soon to cross it in arms.

The Convention, specially called to pass upon the grave subject of secession, sat daily in the Capitol, and the citizens were absorbed in its debates, though business went on as usual; the city looked bright and attractive, the streets resounded with the cry of the melodious "charcoal" hucksters, who seemed at least to be ubiquitous, and the fine, balmy weather plentifully brought out the buds and flowers of spring. All at once came news of Beauregard's firing upon Fort Sumter; hope nearly vanished. A few days after, simultaneously with the news of Lincoln's calling out seventy-five thousand troops, sped Richmond's resolution to secede, and the Convention, hesitating no longer, passed the ordinance of secession. The die was cast—war had come after all. Stirred

with the deepest feeling, resolutely, heartily, exhibiting only a proper enthusiasm, the city began to gird itself for its share in the brunt of the decreed contest. It was almost a race with the young men to see who would buckle on armor first and enlist for a war which was destined to be the bloodiest and longest since the fall of Napoleon at Waterloo, though inexperience led nearly all to believe that it was going to be a picnic, or a sort of picnic affair.

CHAPTER II.

The various military organizations then existing in Richmond hastened to enlist upon the declaration of war, formally accepted by the passage of the secession ordinance, and foremost among them were the "Howitzers." The original organization of the Howitzers, as a company equipped with four howitzer-guns, was formed, on the 9th of November, 1859, by George W. Randolph, subsequently secretary of war of the Confederacy. During the interval necessary for procuring the guns, the new organization was drilled as an infantry company and did service in the John Brown raid; after the guns were furnished, it devoted itself to acquiring a thorough knowledge in the school of artillery tactics. When the Fort Sumter firing occurred, the Howitzers had temporary headquarters in a large hall

under the large Spotswood hotel, which stood at the corner of Eighth and Main streets. They prepared for active campaigning by night and day drills, and held themselves in readiness for any order that might be given by the governor. Just then a war vessel was dispatched from Washington for the purpose of ascending James river and menacing Richmond, as the federal authorities were not certain that Virginia would finally take up arms, and thus hoped to overawe the belligerent citizens eager for the impending fray. The Howitzers were ordered by the governor to go down the river to meet "the enemy," and proceeded to Wilton, about seven miles down, without however catching the least glimpse of the vessel after a couple of days spent in waiting for it. This little expedition was known as the "Pawnee War," from the name of the war steamer, and passed off as a joke upon the return of the command to its drilling at the Spotswood.

A few days after the secession Convention took its final action, the Howitzers were regularly mustered into the State service, and with alacrity they entered upon the duty of defending the cause that Virginia had made her own. On the 21st of April, 1861, the entire command was marched to the State's military headquarters, that were then located in an old building at the south-east corner of the Capitol square, and presided over by Col. W. H. Richardson, who had long been adjutant general of Virginia. Formed in marching trim, the command left the hotel in the forenoon and marched along Main, Ninth and Bank streets to the aforesaid building, when the mustering formalities were gone through and a countermarch of the young volunteers made to the hotel. There was great eagerness for joining the ranks of the Howitzers, as the artillery branch seemed to exercise a decided fascination, and accordingly their organization was speedily filled

beyond the limits set for the original company. Many of Richmond's youth flocked to it, young men already entered on business, and others, fresh from school and college, who had not started out, all of them constituting a fine, strong, enthusiastic band, which embraced, without any misgivings or calculations as to the future, the career opened up for the entire State. Not a single one of them but looked upon himself as given over and devoted to Virginia, while life should last and his services be needed. The novitiate experience of the raw soldiery was amusing enough while at the Spotswood hotel, amidst preparations for the stern ordeal of service, the drilling, standing guard, saluting of officers, &c.

Having been regularly mustered in, it was necessary for the State authorities to find quarters for them, and so they were ordered out to the Baptist college to organize and receive guns and equipments. On a bright, very warm Sunday morning, the command

went by way of Eighth and Broad to the college, the march constituting its official entrance on active duty. The college building was not so large and improved as at present, but was sufficient to hold persons on the scale that soldiers are lodged—that is to say, packed closely together after sardine fashion. The yard was ample, and afforded an excellent drill ground, on which stood the bright boat-guns and the four six-pounders brought down from the Virginia Military Institute by the cadets, who looked like so many kildees beside the stouter, overcoated Howitzers. Having come by the country roads, the six-pounders were covered with mud, and the Howitzers were requisitioned to give them a washing by hand, with sponge and bucket; the task was most curiously, fastidiously, performed by some of the youngsters, who had never been very familiar with country mud—an element whose close acquaintance they had not long to wait for. General Magruder, of Mexican war fame, was

in command of the post, and, frequently presenting himself on the grounds in full regalia as an ex-federal artillery captain, his presence inspired confidence, together with a certain amount of awe, for of course he was one who knew all about war and its mysteries. The cadets themselves were looked up to as learned in the military science, and their drill and other warlike qualities were unstintingly admired. Guards were set around the college grounds, and "the grand rounds" were punctiliously made, amidst endless mirth evolved out of relieving the sentinels in the wee hours of night; the most intimate boon companions were not supposed to know each other except as grim figures passing the watchword.

After a liberal drilling of the recruits, the organization, very much augmented, was formed into a battalion of three companies, under the orders of Major Randolph. The first company so divided off elected J. C. Shields captain, Dr. William Palmer first lieu-

tenant, Edward S. McCarthy second lieutenant, and R. M. Anderson orderly sergeant. All three succeeded to the captaincy, the last mentioned serving at the close. The first company numbered close on to a hundred members, and the other two were nearly as full. The battalion, being given tents, stores, and wagons, took up its first camp at "Howard's Grove" for a few days, whence it was moved to Chimborazo heights, and there drilled for several weeks. In these early camps around the city, the gay crowd of Howitzers became fairly acquainted with each other and indulged much in games and sports; permits for visiting the city and home attractions, so near and yet so far on account of the exigencies of warfaring, were profusely accorded at this time, when the military picnicking had not put on any very wearisome shape. Lager beer, only recently founded in the capital, and mint juleps, handed down from a remote Jamestownian epoch, were both to be had

in town and only in town, whither many of the gay frolickers made frequent raids, very shrewdly arguing that operations in the field would soon necessarily put an end to their splendid opportunities for sampling "Tom Griffin's" and "Euker's." Right they were.

CHAPTER III.

THIS amateur style of soldiering terminated on the 31st of May, when the first company received orders to take the field in earnest at Manassas Junction, and the second and third companies kept back for the peninsula. About noon on that day the company was embarked, with their guns, on a long freight train at the Central, now Chesapeake and Ohio, railroad station, and, after several hours' delay in starting, left Richmond rejoicing and amid enthusiastic hurrahs for their destination. At the principal stations by the wayside there were crowds to see and greet them—many young ladies, with refreshments in trays and baskets, lavishly supplied, with ice-water and lemonade in abundance. On the next day, June 1st, the Howitzers were landed on the hot plain of Manassas,

when they speedily had their tents pitched and their guns parked. Their battery was the very nucleus of the artillery corps that was to contribute so effectively to the building up of the undying fame of the "Army of Northern Virginia." Things were found very quiet at Manassas; very few troops had reached there, Beauregard was in command, there were rumors of cavalry dashes towards Washington, the weather was extremely hot, the drills heavy and exhausting, but the messes were well supplied, and especially well patronized, thanks to hard exercise and splendid appetites that foreshadowed a consuming drain on Virginia's commissary department. Foraging at that flush and dawn of hostilities was excellent, and the mess-tables, rough-board constructions under the broiling sun, were loaded with the delicacies of the season, over and above the bounteous ration of flour, bacon, beef, molasses, coffee and sugar, regularly issued.

The Howitzers soon made themselves at home, and formed lasting acquaintance with the other commands present—cavalry, infantry, and artillery—especially with a Lynchburg battery that early arrived at the Junction under Captain Latham. Drill was incessant, great stress being laid by the officers on battery drilling with horses in the field, an experience which the company had never before gone through with. Target-firing was also practised, but only occasionally and to a limited extent, as superior orders had been given for the saving of ammunition, which was not abundant—indeed exceedingly scarce—and therefore the commanding general wisely thought it should be reserved, in Wellington's style, for the approach of the foe within short, net range. Amusements under such a scorching sunshine had chiefly to be confined under the shelter of tents, and thus it came about, one may say in the nature of things, that the Howitzers

contracted a very strong habit of lying down on straw to read newspapers and novels, sent from home regularly, and to play cards. The Howitzer mail was ever big; probably they received, from first to last, more letters and newspapers than any other company in the army, and these missives constituted things of beauty and joy, the best kind of "treat." The cry of "——— ———, here's a letter for you!" was an enthusing one anywhere in the woods. It was at Manassas that "euchre" and "seven up" were inaugurated by the Howitzers, though the overwhelming syndicate of "poker" was only fairly started at a later date, on other camping grounds. There were many rare conveniences to be indulged in at Manassas. Several of "the boys" had brought along to the front Saratoga trunks, filled with civilized apparel, white pants, collars, cuffs, and like finery, and in off moments took occasion to sport them. But, being so prodigiously out of place

under the surroundings, a yearning for Richmond's streets and parlors seized several of the youthful wearers. On one occasion, a member of this ultra fashionable set, being vexed at some slight happening, waited upon the captain in his tent and formally handed in his written resignation as a "high private." To his utmost surprise and annoyance, he was officially informed of the meaning of the words "too late," and his feeling of chagrin became deeper when the facts were noised about camp, though the joke was so good that it afterwards merely lingered, a joke and a tradition.

CHAPTER IV.

MANASSAS was easy of access from Richmond, and many visitors came up to inspect things at the seat of war, among them no less a personage than General R. E. Lee, who was then stationed at headquarters in Richmond, and not only unknown to fame (except locally for the part he had played in Mexico), but somewhat under a cloud for the trifling check suffered in West Virginia at the hands of McClellan. General Lee came up to inspect the position militarily, and to report, and of course attracted a great deal of curiosity, though he did not come near to eclipsing Beauregard, the idol of Manassas. General Lee was then about fifty-six years old—a man of fine soldierly bearing in his federal uniform, with only iron gray hair and of comparatively fresh appearance. His mil-

itary aspect and the manner of sitting his horse, erect and a little stiff, were remarked as he rode about, attended by a small staff of young officers; but he was not a "sensation"—only another inspecting officer from Richmond, and of course no one could then dream that he was cut out to be the coming chieftain of the Southern movement.

Towards the close of June the battery, supported by General Bonham's brigade, was ordered by General Beauregard to Fairfax Courthouse as an advance guard against any incursions from Washington, where astute old General Scott was busily preparing for the invasion of his native State. It was a short march over a country that had never felt the heel of war, across the little tree-bordered stream of Bull Run and through the hamlet of Centreville, both looking extremely insignificant, yet on the eve of becoming famous. At Fairfax Courthouse the battery camped on a field a few hundred

yards from the historic and smiling little village, which was forthwith visited and inspected by the cannoneers. Fairfax was a reminder of Washington and many of Virginia's earliest eminent personages, though no one went about to find the precise spot where the Father of his Country was knocked down by a young villager in consequence of a quarrel. There were few stores, but they yet had on hand stocks of goods, and the soldiers proved good customers. It was too small a place for much visiting, and besides the duties of instruction in camp prevented. The neighborhood furnished fresh supplies of all sorts to the soldiers, its freshness and bloom then being untouched, but in a few short weeks to be utterly obliterated by the havoc of battle and occupation of vast armies. Here the Howitzers first put hand to the erection of field earthworks, or "breastworks," as they were commonly called—an occupation that was regarded as tedious

and very hard labor by the city bred youths. The line of these fortifications ran across an extensive open field, fronting the road leading from Washington, so that a fire could be directed, if necessary, upon any column approaching from that direction. The incipient earthworks were of the fanciest kind, built at nice angles, under martinet rules, with sand-bags, fascines, stuffed baskets, and other paraphernalia that would not have been amiss in Julius Cæsar's camps, according to the style of his intrenchments. The labor was thrown away, as far as they could serve, for they were never used; but great zeal was displayed during this instructive exercise in the art of putting up scientific earthworks, which had then become very much in vogue in the military world, thanks to the exceptional example afforded by the siege of Sebastopol and the experiences of the Crimean war. Engineers had conducted things in the Crimea, and Beauregard was a great engi-

neer, and so early set this example of engineering, which style of fighting, based on the defensive system, was adopted for the Confederacy and followed to the last.

The stay at the Courthouse lasted very pleasantly, with intermissions of false alarms and the beating of "the long roll," or call to arms, until the 17th of July, when the head columns of General Scott's army debouched down the Washington road. The glittering bayonets of the winding columns and the white-topped wagons in the early morning sunshine could be distinctly and closely seen right across the field where the Howitzers had put up their earthworks, and where they at once took position, without breakfast for the first time in their warlike life, ready to open fire at command. On came the enemy's columns, without opening fire and leisurely, as if they intended to go on to Richmond without so much as noticing the presence of the "rebels," squatted by the wayside,

and who, from the very outset of the long campaigning, were standing strictly on the defensive, with fire reserved against attack. After a brief spell of hurry-skurry in getting ready for a dignified departure, the battery and supporting brigade headed back towards Centreville and Bull Run, the enemy marching quietly in the rear, though huge pillars of smoke at times showed the Virginians that the invaders had wantonly commenced burning country houses—the first sign of hostilities. The roads were dusty and hot and the battery slowly made its way back, stopping for drinks at the roadside wells, for feeding and resting the horses and men; the march was continued during the night, under strict orders not to light a pipe, not to strike a match, or speak above whispers, as a concealment against any spies that might be lurking in the forest on either side of the way. The war was young indeed then; the soldiers were novices; veterans came later and acted

far differently. A little before daylight Bull Run was reached, along which stream for a considerable distance on the south side General Beauregard had lined strong earthworks to bar the passage to Richmond, intending to deliver battle at that point. Cannoneers and infantrymen were immediately placed in position for fighting along this line, and the army, reinforced and collected, with sharp lookouts, took a little rest, under the warm wave of weather then prevailing, snatched a hasty breakfast, and then calmly began the day's work of waiting for the enemy's arrival.

CHAPTER V.

They did not have to wait in vain on this 18th of July, the day of the combat—a small one, but it was the first serious scrimmage, the precursor of battles on a large scale. Shortly after noon a battery of the enemy's army from the height wheeled out in the open field, near the Centreville road, and, under direction of an officer on a white horse, opened fire on the Bull Run line just opposite, at Mitchell's ford. It was Rickett's battery, celebrated in the old United States army as having taken part in the Mexican war, and it was soon reinforced by an immense rifle piece, which received the name of "Long Tom" on account of its far reaching and accurate firing. The wily Scott, ensconced at Washington and represented on the field by McDowell, had ordered the Bull Run line to be

carefully felt by artillery before venturing to cross it, as the news had got out that "masked batteries" were as thick as blackberries in the woods of the Manassas region. It was a light artillery duel, with small losses, between the two hosts concealed under the cover of the woods, and the Washington Artillery of New Orleans and the Alexandria battery played the principal part in it, the infantry being only slightly engaged. The Howitzer battery, stationed at Mitchell's ford, did not fire a gun during the day, but was exposed to a very searching fire throughout, and its guns were visited by General Beauregard in person, clad in a short sack coat and wearing a light colored felt hat, to make sure that all was in readiness at the crisis of his preparations, in case of an attempted rush at this point of the main road. The crashing and exploding of projectiles, approaching this time in quest of life, not receding beautifully as in target practice, was rather a startling ac-

quaintanceship; the first one seemed to have begun the destruction of the world, and the ones immediately succeeding to be clinching the job; but the unusual roar became a shade more familiar before it ceased with the darkness of twilight. There was a rest until Sunday, the 21st of July, which opened with a warm wave both from the weather clerk and the enemy. The Howitzer battery occupied the same position, did not fire, but were fired upon all during the fight, which swept along the line, with feints here and there, the heavy fighting on the left, where flanking was attempted from early morning until about 5 P. M. It was about this hour that the celebrated "Rebel Yell" took its origin, with an upward, onward and "to be continued in our next" course, as the newspaper editors say. Never a more joyful and clearly ringing sound than that struck the ears of the Howitzers as it first faintly from the distance reached their position, then strengthening

and growing as it came, louder and louder, whirling in the air from the extreme left on down to the right, thrilling, electrifying all with the words "*they're retreating, they're routed!*" The battle was over, the panic had set in, and "On to Washington" had replaced "On to Richmond." Enthusiastic haste was made by the Howitzers in starting out in pursuit, but the roads were encumbered with the enemy's wreck and plunder, cast-off equipments and material, and, as darkness began after proceeding a short distance on the Centreville road, the generals decided not to advance, and the troops were ordered back to their positions along the field which had been consecrated during the day with fire and blood. The Howitzers resumed their "as-you-were" attitude.

Intense elation induced a great many persons, both in and out of the army, to think the war was over. The battle was a decisive one as to the superior generalship and espe-

cially soldiership of the South, and in many ways may now be seen to have exercised an influence in prolonging the war. It was also decisive as to immediate results on the field, for never after was there such another panic and total rout. Visitors poured in from Richmond to see their relatives and the sights, and the correspondents made haste to get their mills grinding. The day following that of the fight was rainy throughout, but this did not prevent the burying of the dead, caring for the wounded, and inspecting the fields. All wandered freely over the slopes and plains, and minutely examined spots and points where the engagement had been fiercest.

CHAPTER VI.

It was the Howitzers' first glimpse of a battle-field, and their curiosity was satisfied in regard to the wounded and dead of the federal host, which had nearly doubled the number of the defenders; but the ground and the varied accounts of the fighting outweighed a thousand fold in interest the mere dead bodies, the strewn relics and freshly-dug graves. The enemy's supplies left in their camps and scattered on the roads were abundant, and a good deal of their finery was secured on the field, such as clothing, blankets, rubber overcoats, knapsacks, canteens, pistols, &c. It was an interesting epoch, and the tales that came back from Richmond and the North were truly entertaining to the Howitzers, who were always fully posted and alive to the times. Indeed, they seemed

through the war to have an intuitive knowledge of operations in advance of their coming off; the newsmongers of the company invariably ferreted out whatever was or was to be with a surprising accuracy and rapidity, because they were endowed with gifts that enabled them to talk on a rare footing with commanding generals.

The battery soon found out that it would be ordered to locate its camp at Centreville, where it sojourned a couple of weeks, protected by tents, which were then plentiful and fashionable. As it turned out, going into camp at Centreville was merely a gentle pastime for playing poker, drilling a bit, talking about the battle, and seeing Prince Napoleon pass by on his visit to Beauregard's headquarters at Manassas. But not even at this camp did the chief occupation of army life, as discovered by so many, apart from marching and fighting, get under full headway, and only at Goose Creek, near Leesburg, did the Howitzers secure a thorough

drill in poker. On one occasion, under the personal direction of Brigadier General Longstreet, the battery had a notable field drill at Centreville, charging as horse artillery in the rear of cavalry. Prince Napoleon, the cousin of Napoleon III., to visit the camp, left his hack on the pike and walked over among the collected crowd of Howitzers, who curiously viewed him in a Napoleonic light and as the possible bearer of peace or glad tidings. Colonel Skinner, of the first Virginia regiment, explained to him in French the topography and exploits, and then his corpulent and serene Highness bore away towards Manassas Junction. On his return for Washington, the battery was drawn up in parade order along his route to do him the honors.

The opening of August was extremely oppressive, and the Howitzers were not sorry when ordered to pack up their traps—and at that early day these were numerous—

and join General Evans' brigade, stationed at Leesburg. The march was rapidly accomplished, the cannoneers walking in fatigue dress and order, and occasionally managing to secure a ride on horse, limber chest or caisson, the route pleasant, and food liberally supplied at the country houses passed. The first camps of the battery at Leesburg were of a temporary character; two of the guns were left on the east side of the town, two placed on the west. Two, the left section, were stationed at "Big Spring," an immense pool of running water, big enough to float a small schooner, clear and ice cold, and of great convenience to thirsty soldiery. Leesburg was very attractive as a place for visiting "the ladies," purchasing knick knacks, getting a square meal at the hotels, and afterwards, for a rarity and variety, sitting in the porches in good old hotel style. Leaves to visit town were unstinted; it had a few bar rooms and a large assortment of

stores. While stationed in separate camps, "the sections" frequently skirmished with the enemy along the Potomac river, as far as Loudon Heights, and in this service first had occasion to use with good effect their guns. Some of the routes followed, especially the one over the Blue Ridge to Berryville, afforded fine marching, though getting into position on the crest of the hills was attended with some little difficulty. The routes had, so to say, landmarks; years after the close of the war, the same routes, upon being revisited, seemed to be precisely just in the order they had been at that time—the buildings there, the board fences there, the turns in the road, the same piles of husks, the same cattle and individuals, all with a familiar, home like, steady appearance.

CHAPTER VII.

WHEN the battle of Leesburg took place, on the 21st of October, the battery was reunited, and occupied a point near the bank of the river where the enemy crossed and fought, but the nature of the ground and close quarters of fighting did not admit of artillery firing, and so the Howitzers took no other than an expectant part. But the affair yielded them a large stock of supplies and trophies, chief of which was a brass rifled cannon, with new fangled ammunition, that General Evans gave them for incorporation with their organization. It was manned and attached as the "fifth gun," but it proved in a short while to amount to nothing more than a "fifth wheel on a coach," and was dropped out and off the list. Here many Belgian muskets were captured, and from the ground were

picked up by all comers, but finally dispatched to the shops at Richmond for use. Firing at fences and barn doors with Belgian muskets was quite a sport for some days after the remnants of the enemy's force that had visited old Virginia's shores had got back on the other side of the river. As a renewal of the crossing, in greater force, to support this pretended "reconnaissance," was looked for, the brigade at Leesburg, with the battery, was withdrawn by General Beauregard's orders, a few miles back, in better reach with Manassas. No renewal was made, and, after a few days spent in the backwoods, where an extraordinary supply of "chain lightning" suddenly gushed forth as if by magic, the position was resumed at Leesburg, to the great delight of the Howitzers, who had become warmly attached to the place and had been grieved to withdraw and leave the hospitable citizens and fair ladies to the threatened incursion. The speedy return made

all things well again, and seemed to double the happiness of citizens as well as of soldiers.

The "left section" was posted for the winter in an elevated earthwork named Fort Evans, overlooking the river, and the "right section," or the greater part of the enlarged battery, was sent to encamp at Goose Creek to guard the turnpike in the direction of Washington; and here it spent the winter, with occasional raiding up to the mountains. Goose Creek was the most famous camp the Howitzers had during the war. It lasted long, the times were early and good, provisions were abundant in Loudon—a county proverbially rich and overflowing in agricultural products—paper money was worth something on the dollar, boots made of excellent leather by hand and to order were purchasable, Leesburg was exceedingly attractive, and the mails were uninterrupted. Soldiers were never granted a softer, pleasanter breathing spell in war or peace.

Duties were light, in reality there were no duties at all; a sweet-to-do-nothingism possessed the whole "band of brothers" gathered in that little stumpy, tree-girt spot by the Dranesville pike. The cannoneers were ready to do whatever was bid—all they could; but there was nothing to do.

CHAPTER VIII.

Going after hay for the horses, "hay details," and putting up "breastworks," ordered by General D. H. Hill, when the fall of Fort Donelson enthused him to order them, simply afforded some of the finest fun, chaffing and laughter, any soldiers ever had. Yes, there was something to do, too. Play-poker. The camp now took up this business in earnest, and though it was transacted on the credit system and never panned out on a cash basis, the task of perfecting themselves in it proved to many of the novices to be the most arduous of all their experiences. There were a few passed-masters of the art, who were at special pains to indoctrinate them, but success was difficult to gain. Enthusiasm was steady, the business went on day and night, without intermission, for eating and camp

calls were shifted as much as possible, for the purpose of keeping a winning or a losing hand and letting the game go on. Grains of corn invariably represented the stake, and, for the most part, were the only stake played for, as few were ever "redeemed" by the "bank," or any one else. The paymaster only visited the place once during the winter, the sole and last time some of the Howitzers ever saw him; indeed, a few of them never did see him from beginning to end of their service, and, notwithstanding that they long ago cheerfully waived their dues, remain as ever legally entitled to draw on the Confederate Treasury. Log huts, protected by "tent flies," afforded comfortable, snug dwellings, and an immense fire, constantly fed by huge hickory, oak, and pine trees, roared on the open ground about which the dwellings were collected. This outdoor fireplace was for standing and sitting around on benches. Kitchens and mess tables, presided over by

hired negro cooks, were run on the outskirts of the camp, with regular hours for meals and cow bells for summoning the boarders.

The earthworks playfully put up at Goose Creek were small, remarkably light, speedily terminated, and then left to the tender mercies of the trees, birds, and weather—the whole job performed out of all possible likelihood for use, yet a source of innocent merriment. Entertainments were frequently got up in and around Leesburg for the benefit of the Howitzers. In the beginning of the encampment at Goose Creek, explorations were made in the neighborhood as to the item of diversions, and the rumor circulated that there was a place called "Fiddler's Green," just across the creek, which enjoyed a high reputation, and at once it assumed the most extensive and fanciful proportions in the eyes of the young frolickers. The very name, "Fiddler's Green," was a fascination. Runners reported progress on a most lively scale, and its

fame increased as it went from mouth to mouth, until it became a camp-word for all, a mystery to some. In reality it was merely a small shanty, owned by a widow woman with three grown daughters, all of whom played on the fiddle, and the establishment sold snacks, groceries, and "moonshine whiskey." It was a veritable bonanza. Some of the frequenters immediately got up a grand ball. Preparations for "The Ball" were the talk of the camp; the invited arrayed themselves as gorgeously as possible to do honor to the affair, which passed off more than pleasantly, with incessant outbursts of "anger-pray-bury" jollity. An extra fine supper was spread in the buffet style, as there was no table sufficiently ample or chairs enough to go round in the throng limited to standing room only. Moonshine flowed freely and dancing was continuous. Drinks were not few or far between during the whirling tournament of reels, jigs, quadrilles, waltzes, lancers,

polkas. Each dancer vied with the other in cancan pedotechnics, and the fun went on from the unfashionable ball-hour of dewy eve until the dawn of day, when the guests disbanded and made their way back to camp as well as they could on foot. Several of them fell in the creek on the return trip without any damage, on the contrary, and those who were sufficiently restored on reaching camp pictured "The Ball" as the embodiment of fairyland. Fiddler's Green and its ball remain a vivid, unfading Howitzer reminiscence.

CHAPTER IX.

In March, 1862, in accordance with General Johnston's strategic plan of withdrawing the army from "Northern Virginia" to Richmond, the battery took up its line of march homeward, together with the detached brigade. While at Leesburg, Captain Shields resigned, and Lieutenant Palmer was "elected" to take command. Leesburg was again evacuated, to the regret of both sides, and all of the material collected there, as at Manassas and Centreville, that could not be carried off, was delivered over to the flames. Parting with the citizens was sorrowful, and a decided air of gloom, increased by the burning heaps, settled over the place at the moment of the start, which was made in the night so as to conceal the movement from the enemy's lookout on the Maryland side of the

river. Yet the Howitzers were joyful at the prospect of getting home, of entering upon active operations, for they had been stationed at Leesburg over six months. They began their long march from the Potomac to the James in rather gay spirits and in most excellent condition. They had become in a measure seasoned, and no soldiers knew better how to get along and make the most of circumstances. Their city-bred acquirements had now been fortified and developed by rude life in the bracing, suggestive country. Marching they had reduced to a science after such a protracted stretch of tramping about; all its intricacies had been mastered, and the way of getting over the most ground in the shortest time and with the least wear and tear seemed to have become an intuition with them. They knew when to go and when and where to stop; they knew what to tote and what to leave aside, never burdening themselves with accoutrements; when and how to get

rides and when to foot the route for special purposes, and country houses, with varying degrees of comforts and delicacies, they could most unerringly spy or snuff from afar. Of springs and wells they kept posted, and possessed better than a general's eyes for commodious camping-grounds.

CHAPTER X.

HEADED for dear old threatened Richmond, they made good headway, their speed only slackened by orders from army headquarters. The routes were familiar, having been often travelled over; their friends and acquaintances were numerous, and their "calls" likewise; well received everywhere, their coming was sometimes anticipated and prepared for. Muddy or dry roads, weather stormy or bright, all was one, and the camping-ground by the wayside ever resounded with the gleefulness of this band of young Virginia stalwarts—happier than they knew during these their none-such moments. A stop—a halt for accidents or rest for beast and man—horses being entitled to first consideration, and lo! see there that chirpy, lively cannoneer step out in a green wheat-field, somewhere, anywhere, start a fire, haul out from his

little canvas bag, smaller than a lady's satchel, a provision of coffee and sugar, and brew a small pot of coffee equal to the best French dripped, for the restoration of himself and special friends, attracted to the spot without any calling, who all the while gazed admiringly on at the operation. It was simply the ordinary achievement of some thoughtful "brewer of coffee," hugely enjoyed as far as it went. Special providences of this kind abounded, in more ways and lines than one, to help out a march or the toughest scenes of actual hostilities. These adaptations, akin to the generous, soldierly spirit prompting to divide a cup of water or crust of bread with a comrade, to care for his wounds or bury him, were followed out into the nicest ramifications. Down through Middleburg, skirting Manassas Junction, through Berlin, Little Washington, Culpeper Courthouse, and Orange Courthouse, where the hotels were patronized, and "set," but much deteriorated, meals

were procured for an ever-increasing supply of printed paper, and where the red mud and mire stuck deep and ,thick, on by way of Gordonsville and Hanover Junction to the outskirts of home, but not yet at home on account of military discipline. "Captain, can I go into Richmond? I want to see them all at home mighty bad!" This was now the eager demand during a short halting, and then the battery found itself, parked at "Camp Lee," within still easier range. The greetings and pleasures of home appeared on the boards positively for a few days only. General Magruder was hard pressed at Yorktown, and the Howitzers, with the bulk of the A. N. V., had to hasten forward to relieve this pressure by McClellan's forces already landed on the peninsula. The battery was happy and proud over the greetings it received when it marched, in its best order, through Richmond's streets to Rocketts to take the steamer for conveyance down the river.

CHAPTER XI.

ONCE landed on the peninsula, the cannoneers saw at a glance that there had been indeed a change in their fortunes; that they had at last fallen upon a very tough district—aye, marry, into a mousetrap, as it were. But this was merely a solid perception—nothing more. On reaching the line of fortification that ran directly across the peninsula to Yorktown, the battery went into camp at the point selected for it and began its duties. General Magruder, with a brilliant staff, honored it with a special visit of inspection. The region might have been called swampland—naturally so, rain or shine, no matter; pretty uncomfortable for our Leesburg rose-bud-wearing landlubbers, thus hurriedly compelled to get on sea legs. Puddles, lakes, creeks, morasses, mud, huge stumps, logs, and

trees, decayed monsters, fallen or cut from the time of Captain John Smith, or possibly Powhatan's remote ancestry—all this had to be butted up against in night marches through the forest, obstacles that called rather for the fine dealing of owls and cats. While at this camp Captain Palmer resigned, and Lieutenant McCarthy was "elected" in his place. It was a comical sight to see the officers of an army "elected" by the people in ranks. From the camp to Dam No. 1, some little distance, these obstacles lay in the way of the gun detachments as they relieved each other in turn. Dam No. 1 was the particular angle of the fortified line under a severe fire for several days from McClellan's batteries, within close range, all the warmer as the general Confederate policy was invariably to be saving in ammunition, there being none to waste or throw away, because so scarce and difficult to get or make under the bonnie blue flag. When the line was abandoned by

General Johnston, the battery welcomed its orders to withdraw and to again take its march toward Richmond, over a short and pleasant route to Williamsburg, where a quiet rest was indulged in during several days.

CHAPTER XII.

THE enemy's vanguard reached the neighborhood of the earthworks, previously erected by General Magruder around Williamsburg, before the battery started to leave its camp in the village, and it immediately hurried to Fort Magruder to check the approach. While galloping forward, the cannoneers running at full speed on foot beside the guns, General Johnston and his staff were passed, when he turned and shouted: "Hurry up with your guns," words that added to their speed and enthusiasm. Before occupying the works, the battery wheeled in the open field near by and fired several rounds upon the advancing calvary and sharpshooters, who thus were effectually driven back. The next day, May 5th, the battle occurred under a drizzling sky, and the battery in Fort Magruder was ex-

posed to a heavy front and enfilade fire, and to sharpshooters, but promptly repulsed every attempted advance of the enemy in front. This was its first active engagement in battle. The earthworks, entirely unconcealed by woods, were rendered difficult through the mud and rain, but this kind of drawback had now grown to be familiar to the cannoneers as an accompaniment to the roar of battle. They felt at dark that they had contributed to the glorious little victory, the substantial checking of the invading columns, and the same night they withdrew to Williamsburg and slept in deserted lofts and barns in the outskirts—admirable quarters after the trials just passed through. The march was resumed early next morning over the muddy route, much cut up by the previous passage of large bodies of troops—foot, horse, artillery, and wagons, and after some days of retreating the battery camped just below and in the neighborhood of Rich-

mond. Of course permits to visit it were freely bestowed, and still more freely used, for though the Howitzers punctiliously adhered to and obeyed the spirit of military discipline, they were not indisposed to encroach upon its letter when they regarded such a course to be perfectly legitimate. They did not need to be strict disciplinarians, to be held or bound as such; no tribute, but all for self-government was their cardinal maxim. Hence, whenever the battery fetched up anywhere in the proximity of Richmond, there was no little "running of the blockade" (a phrase incidental to the permanent state of the Confederacy)—and some of the more eager, when on the line immediately below town, found it convenient to run into it nightly. "When I was around Richmond," quoth one, "I kept a horse and came in regularly every night!" "I had an officer's coat, without the insignia of rank, and it always managed to pass me at our general's headquarters; I

lent that coat out, I believe, to nearly every member in the company!" quoth another. Very often in camp an order would be issued, when the privates would unceremoniously walk into the captain's tent and discuss it with him, and, if the order did not hail from outside headquarters, it was changed to suit the judgment of the claimants. If any example of discipline was at any time made out of a Howitzer, it invariably was due to the exaction of some general officer on the march. An instance of this kind was afforded during the Sharpsburg campaign, when several very young Howitzers were caught, contrary to orders, as they emerged into the road from a foraging expedition to a house near by. A general officer at once ordered them to shoulder fence-rails and march under the broiling sun for some distance with their load, burdensome enough for delicate fellows as they happened to be, particularly one of them, Frank Arents, who

was very young and small in size.
Frank, gleeful and radiant with boyish mischievousness, was ever as ready for fun as for duty, but discipline in a trifling matter of capturing a fine, big turkey was something he had never looked out for, and he was very glad to throw off his fence rail when the word of command was given, along with the fatherly admonition "not to do so any more."

CHAPTER XIII.

This promiscuous visiting was put in abeyance by the battle of Seven Pines, and the series that began on the 26th of June. On the 31st of May, the enemy having concentrated along the Chickahominy river, the opportunity of battle was presented to General Johnston, who immediately seized it for attacking, and, but for his wounding and other miscarrying occurrences, a more complete success would doubtless have resulted. The battery, now serving in combination with others and large masses of troops, took part in this as in the subsequent fights, under General R. E. Lee, newly appointed, at Mechanicsville, Cold Harbor, Gaines' Mill, Savage Station, and Malvern Hill. In marching and fighting through the tangled belt along the Chickahominy, trying hardships and privations, hun-

ger, loss of sleep, fatigue, pain and sorrow as well as joy and victorious shouts fell to the lot of the Howitzers, and they emerged from these famous fields as full-fledged veterans, with an experience that afterward bore them in good stead. Such battles, such scenes as those of the war, were first-class educators—imparters of a knowledge beyond all college cramming, above the power of books to bestow. Another rest was secured by the battery after the protracted fighting near Richmond. Attached to Cabell's battalion of Artillery, McLaws' Division, and united with Jackson's and Hill's corps, it accompanied the army under General Lee into Maryland, where it was conspicuously engaged at the battle of Sharpsburg. The short campaign in Maryland was attended only with the usual humdrum life of the soldier on duty, marching incessantly and putting up with all kinds of privations and emergencies through absolute necessity, with no alternative but endurance. The bat-

tery was encamped in Pleasant Valley while Jackson and Longstreet were negotiating for the reduction of Harper's Ferry, Generals D. H. Hill and Garland holding Rockfish Gap. After the surrender of Harper's Ferry, the battery, with the army, crossed the Potomac at Shepherdstown. On the night of the second day's fighting at Sharpsburg the army withdrew from that obstinately-contested field and the battery recrossed into Virginia. After slow marching and frequent camping, it proceeded to the banks of the Rappahannock, to oppose Burnside's advance, or the third "On to Richmond" movement, and arrived at Fredericksburg during a cold nor'easter rain. The smooth routine of camp life there was not of long endurance, and on the 13th of December the two opposing armies joined battle. The battery was posted behind earthworks near Marye's Heights, and, though exposed to a galling fire in the early part of the day, was not actively en-

gaged, as it was not thought expedient to fire from that point upon the advancing foe. General Barksdale, picketed at the outset on the river front, and suffering from the enemy's artillery and sharpshooters, sent for a section of the battery to support him, and it accordingly started out to his assistance, but, meeting on the way with General McLaws, he remarked that "no artillery can live where you are going," and ordered it to return to the line of earthworks. The victory won, the battery went at once into winter quarters.

CHAPTER XIV.

The Howitzers' winter quarters were during each of the four memorable winters most comfortably rigged out. Their style of architecture was by far more useful than ornamental. Canvas or board roofs over small log cabins, having brick, wood, or mud chimneys, were readily put up, as the cannoneers had made themselves expert in building, and wood was ever close at hand, to be had for the cutting. Good cabins and good fires never lacked, and, whatever else might lack, there was always plenty of Virginia's staple "weed" for smoking in camp. Some of the improvised dwellings were more tasty than others, some extremely queer, but all were very snug for use, with bunks, containing straw or bushes for sleeping accommodation, and, above all else, they resounded

with an endless flow of cheerful contentment or playful gaiety. Winter quarters were oases in the barren waste of war; the two singled out by general consent as the most agreeable were Goose Creek, near Leesburg, in 1861, and Morton's Ford, on the Rapidan, in 1863. As a member was often wont to remark, most complacently, during the actual course of his marching and camping: "No command in the army is more fer-tile in resource for entertaining itself than the first company of Howitzers!" Truly, its members did possess in an eminent degree varied accomplishments. Some were musicians and sang in glee-clubs. The aforesaid member used, in his spare moments, to call upon one of his singing comrades: "Ned, I think you've the finest tenor voice I ever heard in my life; sing that song, 'Moon behind the Hill,' I think it's the sweetest thing I ever heard in my life!" Some were card-players, of whom the admirer of "Moon behind the Hill" was

the chief, which rank invariably kept him the busiest inmate in winter quarters. Whilst some were literary in their tastes. The latter read everything they could lay their hands upon; but that was not much, exception being made of "*Les Miserables*," which persistently turned up in every camp-ground throughout the army during the two last years, Victor Hugo's spirited sketch of Waterloo was an attraction, and, besides, the book was about the only one, certainly the only readable one printed in the Southern Confederacy. There was no way or excuse for lugging literature around on the march. The detachments allotted to each gun of the battery were numbered first, second, third, and fourth; they were also given a certain rank, on the score of their peculiar qualifications, by "public opinion," which was powerful in the company. The first detachment was rated as "highly moral swells," the second as "musicians and æsthetical critics,"

the third as "pirates, gamblers, outlaws," the fourth as "a school of philosophers, learned in all the arts and sciences, bold to discuss and dispute anything."

CHAPTER XV.

On the 30th of April, 1863, Hooker crossed the Rappahannock, and fortified with strong earthworks at Chancellorsville, within half a mile of the river, and this move was promptly met by General Lee's army. Active operations, after the long winter rest, were resumed by the Howitzers. Their four guns bore a prominent part in firing, with very damaging effect, upon the retreating forces when they rushed to cross the river and get back to their muddy encampment on the Stafford side.

Chancellorsville was the last victory of Stonewall Jackson, the most splendid effort in the short but ever memorable career of this great hero, who was idolized by the whole army and by none more admired and appreciated than by the Howitzers, who were present on the field where he

first achieved a name, and also near by the spot where he fell to rise no more. The country around Chancellorsville, a wilderness of forest and undergrowth, was well calculated to conceal the enemy's fortifications, and at the same time admirably adapted to screen the direction of an attack upon him. Lee, with his army, was at Fredericksburg. Jackson was ordered forward, and on the 1st of May he vigorously attacked the enemy's forces deployed in front of his fortified works, and pressed the attack until the impregnable character of these works became apparent. Meanwhile Lee arrived on the scene, and a consultation was held in regard to the further plan of action. Jackson was the first to see at a glance the field open for a supreme exhibition of his usual strategy, with a decisive victory for result. As it was clearly out of the question to attack in front, Jackson proposed to attack in flank, and suggested that he should make a detour of six miles, and then, under

cover of the forest, suddenly swoop down on Hooper's right and rear at Chancellorsville. Lee immediately gave his sanction. The origination and execution of this bold movement was Jackson's greatest achievement, and Lee, in his own handwriting, attributed the victory to this successful piece of strategy.

From the first of his battles, Jackson had been partial to this kind of manœuvre, a partiality that sprang from his fertile and dauntless mind and the thickly wooded country in which the military operations were generally conducted, and which inclined the opposing armies, when face to face for battle, to fortify their respective fronts by a line of earthworks. Jackson, alone of all the generals, adopted the rule, as simple as it was daring, of marching around the opposing earthworks in order to get at his opponents, on unprotected ground and equal chances. To this main point, then, his movements converged through a series of calcula-

tions as nicely conceived as they were accurately carried out. His last flank movement was begun on the morning of May 2nd. Hour after hour, over winding paths and through dense jungles, he toiled forward, at the head of his corps, so skilfully and silently that, up to the last moment, the enemy, engrossed by the demonstrations in front, did not so much as suspect his design. Finally, at a quarter past five in the evening, Jackson gave the order of attack and his troops rushed ahead with their accustomed yell. The charge, as sudden as it was unlooked for, was decisive. Scarcely any resistance was opposed to the sweeping fire and rapid charge of the advancing forces, amongst whom Jackson rode, pointing ahead and exclaiming: "Press forward! press forward!" The pursuit lasted over two hours, or until further headway was stopped by a heavy abatis of trees.

Shortly after this obstacle was encountered, or about 10 o'clock at

night, Jackson, with his staff, rode a little ahead of his lines, in order to reconnoitre; for, in spite of the darkness and the tangled undergrowth, he had determined upon pressing his advantage by swinging his corps around and interposing it between the river and the enemy's army, so placing the latter between two fires— his own and that of Lee. For this purpose he wanted, as he afterward said, "one more hour of daylight;" indeed, his plans for completing the victory were known when he fell, but, to those who succeeded in command of his corps, they seemed impossible of execution and were not attempted, and only he himself could have removed their seeming impossibility and actually applied them under the circumstances. The distance between his own corps and the forces he had been pursuing was only two hundred yards, and he soon found himself in advance of his own troops, without a thought of danger, but bent only on the idea that a great result de-

pended upon his inspecting the ground with his own eyes. Being warned, he quickly remarked: "The danger is all over, the enemy is routed; go back and tell A. P. Hill to press right on." He had advanced more than a hundred yards beyond his troops, when, suddenly, without any conceivable cause, a heavy volley was fired by his own infantry, apparently directed at him and his escort, scattering the party. Jackson turned into the forest and galloped about twenty steps, when he came upon more of his infantry in the attitude of kneeling to repel cavalry, under the notion that a cavalry charge was being made on them in the dark. They fired a volley, and by this fire he was wounded in three places: one ball entered his left arm two inches below the shoulder-blade, shattering the bone and severing the main artery; a second passed between the elbow and wrist of the same arm, and a third pierced through the palm of his right hand. In his helpless condition his horse ran

away with him under a low bough, which tore off his cap and threw him violently backward, though he righted himself in the saddle, seized the bridle with his bleeding right hand, and turned the horse into the road, when one of his staff officers came to his aid and stopped the fugitive animal. The firing ceased as suddenly as it began.

When about to fall from his horse, and being in great pain, he had sufficient strength to murmur the words: "You had better take me down." The officer caught him in his arms as he threw himself forward, and laid him under a tree near the road, when a messenger was despatched for a surgeon and an ambulance. The officer then proceeded to examine his injuries, after removing his field-glasses and havresack, (which contained some paper, envelopes, and two religious tracts,) cutting away the sleeves of the rubber overall, the coat and two shirts from the bleeding arm. Jackson had just remarked to the staff offi-

cer in attendance on him, "Captain, I wish you would get me a skilful surgeon," when General A. P. Hill came up and asked him if the wound was painful. "Very painful," was the reply; "my arm is broken." General Hill pulled off his gauntlets, which were full of blood, and removed his sabre and belt. The arm, now much swollen, was tied up with a handkerchief, and brandy and water were given him to revive his strength. One of the officers exclaimed, in fear of an advance from the direction of the abatis: "Let us take the general up in our arms and carry him off." Jackson faintly and weakly replied: "No; if you can help me up, I can walk." Just at this moment the batteries across the abatis opened with great violence upon the spot, and, amidst a terrific fire of grapeshot and shell, he slowly dragged himself toward his lines. As he passed through them the troops asked, "Who is that?" To this the reply was, "Oh, it is only a friend of ours who is wounded."

The inquiry became so frequent that Jackson said, "When asked, just say it is an officer." He was extremely anxious lest the men about to renew the battle should be discouraged by learning of his wounds, and besought General A. P. Hill and the others not to mention the accident; but the truth could not be kept from them, and their great sorrow and sense of loss dampened their ardor for the conflict.

After a while an ambulance-litter was secured, and he was placed upon it and borne to an ambulance-wagon, amidst a hurricane of shell and canister, during which the litter was once let fall by one of the men, on account of having been shot through both of his arms, when the wounded general fell on his shattered arm, the pain causing him to groan. As he was being borne along he was recognized by one of his division generals, who approached and said: "Ah, general, I am sorry to see you have been wounded. The lines here are so much

broken by the enemy's fire that I fear we will have to fall back." Raising his drooping head, Jackson exclaimed: "You must hold your ground, General Pender! You must hold your ground, sir!" It was his last order on the field. The next day he lay on a hospital bed, just on the edge of the battle-field, listening to the roar of the fighting which was being completed as far as possible under the stunning drawback of his enforced absence. As soon as the wounded general arrived at the field hospital, the chief surgeon, Dr. Hunter McGuire, of Richmond, decided to amputate his arm. Accordingly, he asked, "If amputation is necessary, shall it be done at once?" "Yes, certainly; Dr. McGuire, do for me whatever you think right." The operation was performed, and he went to sleep; on awakening, he asked that his wife might be sent for. He never complained of his wounds, and only referred to them as having been given to him "by Providence" as "one of

the great blessings of my life. I would not part with them if I could." After the close of the battle he was highly gratified to get the following note from General Lee:

"I have just received your note informing me that you were wounded. I cannot express my regret at the occurrence. Could I have directed events, I should have chosen, for the good of the country, to have been disabled in your stead. I congratulate you on the victory, which is due to your skill and energy."

After reading it, he said, "General Lee should give the glory to God."

The presence of his wife, who nursed him until his death, was a source of satisfaction to him. When, finally, she in tears announced to him that his last moments were approaching, he murmured, calmly: "Very good, very good; it is all right." He sent kind messages to his friends and comrades, and expressed a wish to be buried "in Lexington, in the Valley of Virginia." He was delirious a few

brief moments, but finally his excitement ended, his features became serene, and his last words were whispered, with a smile: "Let us cross over the river and rest under the shade of the trees." He died at fifteen minutes past three in the afternoon of Sunday, the 10th of May, from the effects of his wounds, complicated with pneumonia.

In every land the conviction steadily grows that he was the greatest military genius since Napoleon I., to whom he is likened in military brilliancy, as he is to Cromwell in sternness and inflexibility of character. His genius is all the more clearly made manifest in view of the subordinate rank he held and the paucity of means at his disposal. It was genius alone that enabled him to do what he did, in spite of the insurmountable obstacles of a vicious system that beset his path and cramped his progress. Analysis of his generalship indicates that its two distinguishing characteristics were celerity of movement and accu-

racy of calculation. It was with these high tactics that he took the field, and they were synonymous with bold, energetic action, always successfully crowned. Whether acting separately, detached from any supervision on the part of his commander-in-chief, or under the latter's immediate eye, his action was of the same order— evolved out of his own mind, original, never second hand. In each battle his style of fighting bore the unmistakable stamp of his individuality. In the eye of the superficial observer he appeared to take delight in defying established rules; in reality he merely adapted them to his own peculiar way of working; or, rather, took upon himself to extract their good points, and conform to them, while leaving the weaker based on routine. His absorbing study of the art of war led him to choose its vivifying spirit, and to eschew its useless letter, by which his great intuitive perceptions scorned to be fettered. Yet none more than he enjoined strict

military discipline, for all strengthening of discipline he knew to be of value to an army. When his deeds are considered, this thought is constantly suggested: what great results would he not have wrought had he wielded supreme control over the South—what still greater, if he had held in his grasp the ample resources of the North? The campaign in the Valley of Virginia, during the spring of 1862, which sent his name ringing round the world, was war on a small scale, truly—a miniature example of Bonaparte's first campaign in Italy; yet the same in kind, equally as brilliant and marking. But, even for a moment supposing that, if years had been vouchsafed to him, his exploits should have equalled, or surpassed, those of the French genius, he could never have developed into a Bonaparte, for his moral character was of as pure and high quality as his intellect itself. Defiance of law, usurpation of authority, treading on right, could not have possessed a soul like his.

Several members of the Howitzer company had the honor of being taught by Jackson when he was a professor at the Virginia Military Institute, and they had seen him closely. Their souvenirs in connection with these student-days under "Old Jack" were numerous, and proudly they referred back to the good example, the many useful hints of conduct, he set before them. All the cadets whom he had taught were anxious to serve under him in the field, many of them did, and a few were killed in his battles. It was a delight of the cadets who joined the Howitzer company to give a detailed account of his odd ways, to relate feats of his wonderful memory, at the Military Institute. One of these ex-cadets, John Baird, vividly described "Old Jack's" strict method of treating the pupils in the "section-room." "Solemnly, and rather awkwardly seated on his platform, he used to say very little himself, when a cadet was standing before the blackboard. Each was put

through the demonstration of a problem, and compelled to grasp it thoroughly. At his order I sometimes demonstrated the problem to the class, and he gave the closest attention at all of our recitations. Shortly after South Carolina seceded, a misunderstanding between two of the cadets stirred up quite a row among all, and, coming to the ears of 'Old Jack,' he assembled the corps in one of the large section-rooms and made them a little speech, deprecating conflicts between brother cadets, and assuring them of his belief that they would in a short while be called upon to show their fighting qualities in behalf of Virginia. In closing his remarks, he exclaimed: 'And when the sword is drawn,' suiting the action to the word and drawing his own, 'the scabbard should be thrown away!' at the same moment so vigorously throwing away his own that, instead of its falling on the floor, it broke clean through a window pane and dropped to the ground outside.

When we were returning from the Maryland campaign, I fell in with him at the crossing of the Potomac at Williamsport. 'Old Jack' was sitting very erect on his horse in the river, close to the bank, and personally supervising the passage of the army train over a bad part of the water's edge. Dick Wharton (another of 'Old Jack's' cadets) and I were with the battery, near by on the hill, and he proposed that we should go down to the river and have a chat with him, that it would be a great thing, and so forth. I knew 'Old Jack' too well for anything of that sort, and declined to go. 'Well, I'll go and see him,' said Dick, and off he started. A few hours later I saw Dick returning to the battery, bespattered with mud and looking quite disgusted. 'Well,' I asked, 'what did "Old Jack" have to say?' 'Say?' he growled, 'I no sooner spoke to him than he set me to work toting stones and shoveling dirt with the infantry!'"

On the day before the first battle of

Manassas, Jackson with his brigade, drilled in and drawn from the Valley with the rest of Johnston's forces, took position on Bull Run, and, on the morning of the fight, Sunday, July 21st, 1861, he was ordered in haste to the battle field in order to support some Georgians and Alabamians under General Bee, who were slowly but steadily yielding ground in front of overwhelming odds. Learning from a courier that reinforcements were on the way to him, Bee galloped in the direction of the fresh troops and was soon face to face with Jackson at the head of his brigade. Bee, covered with dust and sweat, his sword drawn, his horse foaming, despairingly cried out, "General, they are beating us back!" Jackson betrayed no emotion, but, with a glittering eye, coolly answered, "Sir, we will give them the bayonet." The words electrified Bee, who galloped back to his men, and, pointing to Jackson, shouted, "Look, there is Jackson standing like a stone wall!

Let us determine to die here and we will conquer!" His men rallied beside Jackson's line, which swept forward, first checking, then, at the critical moment, so piercing the enemy's advance as to contribute decisively to the victory. Bee, who was killed, had given Jackson a new name, one destined to become historic, for from that day forth he was to be called only "Stonewall Jackson." After that day his brigade also was called by the name of "Stonewall." When appointed to a separate command in the Valley, his movements were from the outset aggressive. War with him meant fighting as a business. His Valley campaign commenced in earnest about the time McClellan laid seige to Richmond. The aim he had in view was to manœuvre and fight his little force, at first 4,000 men and later increased to 20,000, so as to threaten Washington and prevent the enemy's troops in his front from joining the besiegers, and this aim he carried out in a most masterly manner.

He fought Banks with a double number of troops at Kernstown, and, after being checked, but far from defeated there, slowly retired up the Valley, defeated Milroy at McDowell, and, then being reinforced, again fought Banks, this time at Winchester, and drove him across the Potomac; meanwhile, Shields and Fremont, each with a separate army under command, were despatched for the purpose of forming a junction and capturing Jackson, bag and baggage, but the latter general, by rapid and skilful strategy, managed to pounce upon them before they could unite, defeated Fremont at Cross-Keys and Shields at Port Republic, and thereupon swiftly marched to Richmond and joined General Lee in the attack on McClellan. After the battles around Richmond, Jackson, with a powerful corps, was ordered to repel the advance of Pope, which he did by routing him in battle at Cedar Run, about six miles from Culpeper C. H. The movement was so quickly exe-

cuted that Jackson had got possession of Manassas, with its accumulated supplies, while Pope was confidently fronting Lee many miles away in the rear. Pope hastily turned, at last, and vigorously attacked his daring adversary, who bore the brunt of the tremendous odds against him with characteristic tenacity until Lee, following in his tracks, joined him, when both together routed Pope on the same plain fought over in the preceding year. Now unopposed, Lee invaded Maryland, and sent Jackson to take Harper's Ferry, which he besieged and bombarded so hotly that the garrison, amounting to 11,000 men, with an immense quantity of arms and supplies, surrendered unconditionally. Two days after its capture, Jackson resumed his place in Lee's army to stubbornly oppose McClellan at Sharpsburg. In this campaign the Howitzer battery served in his corps.

CHAPTER XVI.

AFTER Chancellorsville, the battery remained some time in camp near Fredericksburg before starting out on the Pennsylvania campaign. Marching northward, it crossed the Potomac at a point opposite Hagerstown and went to Chambersburg, whence it was ordered to Gettysburg, and on the 1st of July camped within a few miles of the town. On the evening of the 2nd, it took its place in the line of battle and went into action immediately; on the 3rd and 4th it was also engaged, and the artillery, from the confronting heights, exchanged a heavy bombardment from the muzzles of three hundred field pieces. A resumé of the fight, made on the spot by a member of the battery, is the following:—"This was the most important battle, in which was done everything that skill and

undaunted heroism could do. Cemetery Hill was the key of the enemy's position, and General Lee decided to carry it by assault. Pickett's Division, of our corps, Longstreet's, was selected to make the charge. This division had just returned from North Carolina and was in fine condition, its morale high, as its ranks had been freshly recruited. It was a magnificent charge. I was not far off from General Armistead, as that noble old hero, in front of his line, with hat in hand and uplifted sword, gave the word to advance, and stepped forward with a gallantry that drew the admiration of all who saw him, alas! to be instantly killed on entering the enemy's works on the opposite height. The heroic soldiers charged with him up to the works, but, unsupported, were compelled to fall back with heavy losses; they had done their best, but, through some strange fatality, the issue went against them. Upon the miscarrying of this grand charge, the result of

the battle turned. The army entered Pennsylvania with bright hopes; it returned to Virginia with heavy hearts, though with undaunted spirits, ready at any time to meet its opponent and try the gauge of battle. Upon leaving the field, the battery crossed the Potomac, at Falling Waters, and took a short rest on getting back upon Virginia soil."

CHAPTER XVII.

AFTER Gettysburg, many amusing incidents attended camp life during the homeward march. At camp "Poison Field," a mock duel between two members of the battery came off, an affair that may best be narrated in the language of one of the principals and one of the seconds. Here is the principal's account of its origin:—

"The duel occurred in this way. Bill was a fellow who had a knack of finding out, in about a quarter of an hour after the battery went into camp, any house in the neighborhood where there were pretty girls. Near by "Poison Field" he found a house and soon became acquainted with the ladies. Two of the boys and I happened to go there on a 'whacking' expedition, and, on entering the parlor, we saw Bill unceremoniously run out into the kitchen

where he fretted the moments away while we talked with the young ladies. On the return to camp, I sent Bill a challenge, alleging that his failure to introduce us was an insult, his conduct at the house unbecoming a Howitzer, and demanded the satisfaction due from one gentleman to another under the circumstances. The challenge was promptly accepted."

His second gives the details as follows:—

"Bill was in dead earnest in accepting the challenge of Tom, who had agreed to act as a pretended opponent on the occasion, and lent himself admirably to the adaptation of the part. Bill was of a kind to become readily saturated with any idea, and, when so possessed, would swallow anything. His second convinced him that the matter was no child's play, and told him that his opponent was exceedingly wrathy, and that his second had been a Kansas Jayhawker and could cut the hoops off a barrel rolling down a steep hill. I drew up

the programme. Three shots were to be exchanged, at the end of which, if both were alive, they were to draw sabres, advance, and fight to a finish. The preparations were made. My principal was extremely anxious to discover if the balls loading the pistols, were genuine dough, blackened, as had been agreed upon between the seconds, and, the better to assure himself, struck a pin through them, to find out if the dough was soft enough to spread on coming out of the muzzle, 'for,' he remarked, 'it might sting.' Satisfied on this point, a horse was bled to furnish coloring for his shirt front instantly after the firing should cease, the two men were placed in position, and the weapons handed to each. Ostensibly the duel was to be private, but, when it came off, the Howitzer company and the whole of Barksdale's brigade were on the hill to see it. At the third shot, according to previous arrangement, Tom clapped his hand to his breast, and, com-

pletely saturating his shirt with blood, fell. Bill's second said to him: 'You have made a line shot!' I remarked to my principal: 'Steady yourself; die like a man!' The fight thus ended, Tom was taken off the field on a stretcher, when Bill was prevailed upon, without the least difficulty, to witness the dying moments of his unfortunate comrade and opponent. Entering the tent, he extended his hand and said: 'How are you, Tom, old fellow?' Whereupon Tom vigorously shook the proffered hand, and, in his peculiar voice and noted way, replied: 'Very well, I thank you, Wil-liam, how are you?' Bill at last grasped the joke, but it required some diplomatic tact all around to pacify his offended dignity."

CHAPTER XVIII.

THE battery slowly returned Richmondward, for the fourth time, by easy marches, to Gordonsville, where it spent some weeks, and then went into camp near Orange C. H. At the beginning of cold weather, just after Meade's futile movement along Mine Run, the winter quarters of the battery were established at Morton's Ford, on the Rapidan river, about eight miles below Orange C. H. Winter quarters at this point lasted five months, or until the opening of Grant's campaign, and were thoroughly enjoyed. The ground was admirably selected in the edge of the forest, between which and the enemy's encampment on the opposite side intervened a broad expanse of open field, through its midst running the little Rapidan river, picketed by both armies. About a couple of hun-

dred yards off from camp, on the most elevated ground of the line of earthworks, the four guns were kept night and day in position ready to sweep the plain at a moment's notice, and the cannoneers stood guard constantly over them. This was their chief military duty, and, discipline being unusually relaxed, life in the camp was free and easy, spent in the endeavor to extract from the situation all the comfort and amusement possible for whiling the idle moments away. A soldier's life, despite its fair share of ennui, had grown to be almost second nature with the Howitzers by this time, and was made the most of. Every legitimate expedient was availed of for getting over that portion of wearysomeness unavoidably attached to it. Furloughs were granted by General Lee, and many were thus enabled to pass short moments at home. Christmas eve saw even a few adventurers, without leave or license slip off from camp and run at a break-down gait to the train at

Orange C. H., solely for the pleasure of passing the holiday at home. Their roll call absences were excused in view of the irresistible attractions of the holiday times. The winter structures were varied, as usual, some half-tent, some logs, but all with chimneys, and furnished with deftly made "beds," tables and chairs, the outcome of that same ingenuity and industry which was so keenly taxed in civil life, in the homes of the cities and towns. Perhaps the most original military product was "sassafras tea"; the Howitzers managed to have their native dish of bacon and greens by substituting "dandelions" for the greens. Pipes were curiously carved out of hard wood and roots, clothing and spreads were remodeled, the forest was called upon to supply food in the way of game, the fields "stray vegetables" which, when found, were accepted as unadulterated delicacies. "Hay detail," or requisitioning the neighboring farms for horse feed, being a necessary labor,

could not be dispensed with, and, though a little irksome at times, particularly when inflicted as a punishment, was viewed as a pretty sure chance for getting a house dinner somewhere or raw material for the camp mess. A detail of two men and a driver with a four horse team were sent out on these excursions, or rather intrusions, generally over wretchedly cut up roads, and many were the amusing accidents and incidents connected with them. Some fun was to be had out of most any occurrence, the ready soldiers being never at a loss, and none the less tickled when the hay was spilt by the way and the unburdened team and bespattered, weary "detail," tramped back to camp, minus all save a few remnants to show. The hay was taken, or "impressed" on official i. o. u. tickets issued by the quartermasters, and this impressment was a heavy drain on the farmers; nevertheless the Howitzers managed to keep in their good graces, to secure the best fare in their

dwellings, and to make themselves thoroughly entertaining to the household family before quitting it. The farmers would help to load the wagon with the hay, while the family got up a good dinner for the "detail." In spite of such frequent ravages, the "details" were invited to call again and again, till no more hay was left. The exceptional powers exhibited by the cannoneers in entertaining their hosts, under the vexing run of military operations, were ever amply repaid. The "calls" required occasionally no little tact to be successful; now and then, a farmer was stumbled across who seemed at first to be of impossible appeasement. On one special occasion, a farmer, whose native generosity had been soured by bad treatment, was called upon by a "hay detail" of the keenest kitchen-trail. Nothing would do in the way of ordinary politeness. He pronounced all soldiers to be vandals, devils incarnate, and the "detail" chimed in with each and every partic-

ular one of his utterances. The A. N. V. was about the worst for destruction that ever bore arms. These trivial objections were finally flanked and utterly routed by the united assaults of the "detail." Was the gentleman in need of having the wood on his wood pile cut, or of water from the spring? Yes, well then, here be good turns indeed to be done, and, without any ado, the "detail" gracefully and zealously did them for him, and words and acts combined worked wonders on the larder, brought out its very best. This special "detail" often afterwards alluded to this occasion as having set a model of perfect deportment under difficulties, and, whenever these were met at the threshold, this discourse was pronounced: "Well, ——, we will have to do to-day as we did at 'Count Feeaskie's.' I cut a cord of wood that day, and you brought a barrel of water from the spring, which was a mile off, before the old man got pleased and invited us to dinner in his house, where we

found a Georgian with his gun in the kitchen. We got as fine a dinner as we ever got anywhere, and we may get another to-day, if we just set right to work about it."

CHAPTER XIX.

Towards the close of January, 1864, the enemy crossed the Rapidan, at Morton's Ford, for the sole purpose, as he gave out after being driven back, of making another of his noted "reconnaissances in force." The Howitzers were not caught napping, for their own trusty sentinel at the guns, with sharp eyes and ears, sensitive to any operatic rataplan-plan-plan sound, gave the alarm at once, in the early morning dawn, as soon as he spied the enemy's columns descending to cross the ford. The cannoneers rushed to their respective posts of duty, the guns were pointed and steadily fired on the approaching masses, regardless of the artillery firing from the opposite slope. The line of earthworks was manned by General Ewell's corps, which repulsed the attacking infantry, after a sharp ac-

tion around an old barn and dwellings, where the invaders sought some shelter, near the river.

The Howitzers were frequently visited by members of other encampments; but, as a rule, they themselves, owing to the abundance of their own resources, had little inclination to visit, except in the civil walks of life, mostly wherever stood a country-house with good prospects. Here they were strong. The reason of this was due both to a love of variety, and of something to eat. And everybody was hungry all the time in camp. Soldiers had nothing extra to spare or give, and besides it became worse than a mockery to intrude on a fellow soldier's mess, and put him to the pain of exercising a Chesterfieldian hospitality over a few bacon-rinds and lumps of cornmeal. The good things were away over the hills, out of camp, far from the madding crowd of "Lee's Miserables." For young ladies' society, or any manner of good cheer and table fare, a decided

weakness was shown. It was no rare achievement for the Howitzer, whether on the march, or merely foraging from a fixed camp, to secure first class sleeping accommodations, a real bed, spread with real, not imaginary sheets, and this without any hesitancy or begrudging on the part of a country house owner and his family. Pay, when proper, was offered, but no pay was expected in return for these short sojourns. Money was of very little use, at any time, as no way of spending it was found, and, moreover, paper money having undergone an enormous decrease in value, the paymaster was well nigh invisible.

CHAPTER XX.

It was while the company was encamped at Morton's Ford that a notorious burlesque organization was formed in its ranks, namely, the "Independent Battalion of Fusileers." The Fusileers became well known, and furnished an amusing theme. The Battalion consisted on paper of three companies, their officers and men recruited from the four detachments. In the language of its founder, "the qualification necessary for admission was a love of elegant, luxurious ease, an indomitable energy in resisting everything that pertained to bodily or mental exertion, and the Battalion, therefore, constituted a noble band of warriors who could not be induced to exert themselves in any kind of work. On one occasion, a member of the Battalion was on

guard over four bales of hay; the sparks from his pipe set the hay on fire, and the exertion of putting out the sparks was too much for this valiant Fusileer, and the whole lot of hay was burnt up, whereupon private —— was promoted to a lieutenancy for meritorious conduct displayed in burning up four bales of hay, while on guard, to warm his intellect." In the spring campaign of 1864, the major of the Battalion issued the following special order:

"Special Order. Morton's Ford, April 20, 1864. The commanding officer of the Independent Battalion of Fusileers reviews with pride and pleasure the past conduct of the gallant band of veterans he has the honor to command, and wishes to urge upon all commissioned and non-commissioned officers the importance of perfecting themselves in the manual of whacking, so as to prepare themselves for the ensuing campaign which promises to be one of unusual activity and hardship. Signed by the

major commanding, senior and junior captains and the adjutant."

"Lambert's Cavalry" was organized during the encampment at Morton's Ford, and was an enthusiastic corps. Ben Lambert, as its successful organizer, was elected a "major general" to command the corps, and Wat Dibbrell, Bill Hardy, Frank Arents, Bob McCandlish and Grundy were "colonels" in command of the various regiments. The cavalry was mounted on imaginary horses, or sticks, and its prancing about camp drew crowds; the rearing up of Grundy's horse always elicited unbounded admiration, laughter and cheers. Whenever the camp was tranquil, in moments of the most perfect quiet, the cavalry saw a fit opportunity for turning out to make a terrorizing raid: with frightful yells, and wild cavortings, whip and spur, it would ride roughshod over the silent tents, charging all in its path. Now and then the more peaceful occupants of tents voted the cavalry a nuisance, and, im-

provised as infantry, resisted so vigorously that the cavalry was compelled to fall back, after narrowly escaping destruction. Upon such unlooked for checking, the cavalry, ever ready, would metamorphose itself, temporarily, into a musical band. Then, playing upon fictitious trombones, cornets, drums, it paraded up and down, with diverse sounds and screeches intended to convey the airs of the day, "Bonnie Blue Flag," "Dixie's Land," "Maryland, my Maryland." The leader of the band also diversified the entertainment by executing several solo morsels from grand opera by the old masters, and, owing to this circumstance, his more musically uncouth associates had a way of calling the band "the horse-opera troupe." This particular cavalry corps was not a plagiarism on Stuart's or Wade Hampton's, in fact it was not due to any tendency for caricaturing a different arm of the service, but to an inbred, overflowing, youthful playfulness that needed some

manner of outlet—yes, even through "playing soldier" in front of Mars himself.

Cooking, though so essential to the soldiers' well being, was by no means a pleasant indulgence for the Howitzers when emergencies compelled it. Generally they had hired negro cooks, but, in times of battle, the cooks rarely ventured from the rear to the front, and the cannoneers in the course of several consecutive days of fighting had to depend largely on their own chances for cooking. At times like these, details from each detachment were made to work the frying pan and skillet, and the outcome of their cooking was comical, often disastrous, always unsatisfactory, even in the teeth of a soldier's appetite. Not a member of the company rose to any culinary proficiency. During the battle of Sharpsburg, a member of the third detachment, proverbially bad off in point of cooks and other comforts, was detailed to bake a little corn bread, apparently

a simple operation which should not have heavily taxed his powers: he put the meal in a pan unbeknownly perforated, and the more he watered and stirred the meal, the lower it went until, to his great astonishment, it reached the neighborhood of zero, the ration having leaked out under the board. He was excused from cooking after that. When in camp on the Rapidan, the fourth detachment decided to have a Christmas cake. So, as a philosopher said he had seen cakes made and would undertake the job, the sugar and flour of the mess were turned over to him to handle, and he proudly set to work over it. All his messmates looked on with envy. The flour and sugar were mixed, the dough scientifically worked up, and then dumped in a big skillet expressly borrowed from the "Swell First." Finally the cooking commenced. Two hours passed and the cake began to brown. The day came to a close, and the cake was not done yet. The night wore on, and the

cake became brown at bottom as well as on top, and next morning the cake-maker, declaring it to be a success, said: "Now, boys, to prove that the cake is all right, I'll run a stick through it and you can see the inside!" But the stick would not go through. Then a nail was tried: the nail broke. The cake was taken out of the skillet and fell on the ground like a big rock. The cook, with all his knowledge of the fine arts, whether through forgetfulness or lack of adequate ingredients, had simply produced, after twenty hours' cookery, a Christmas cake that appeared to require a pound of dynamite to break it up. "What became of that cake?" "I think it was fired at the Yankees!" The fourth detachment, graded as a school of philosophy, was of course cut up on disputed points and theories, the cake maker just mentioned being its champion disputer and argue-er. This particular mess discussed all subjects during the day, and they were further han-

dled and disputed over in tent at night: General Lee's campaigns were mapped out for him in advance—all previous mistakes of the generals corrected. Music and art were talked over, any mooted difficulties solved unhesitatingly, and the decisions of the more profound among the dogmatics were regarded as final arbitraments, during the hours of sleep, or until morning renewed the general argumentation before the High Court.

CHAPTER XXI.

The Howitzers broke camp and set out on their last campaign in Virginia on May 1st, 1864. The enemy's forces, now placed under the daring Grant, after having been exercised in grand "sham fights" around Culpeper C. H., suddenly swooped across the Rapidan and delivered battle on the famous field of the Wilderness. The battery marched, by Vediersville and Salem Church, to the line of the fighting at the Wilderness, but, owing to the dense undergrowth there, artillery was out of place, and it could not be used in the action, though standing all the while in ready array. Some of the prisoners, who were made to come out of the bushes and file by the battery, looked like bandbox curiosities, so neat and fresh were their uniforms. From the Wilderness, the march was taken up, along a route strewn with the dead

horses of Sheridan's cavalry, to Spotsylvania C. H. After some moving about there to points specially threatened by the enemy's "flank" advances, it went into permanent position on the line that the circumstances hastily necessitated, and earthworks went up like magic under the bayonet and spade of the infantry, affording in a few hours a very substantial defence. At this point the battery was engaged several days exposed to the fire of artillery and the improved weapons and marksmanship of the sharpshooters, Westerners. Several charges were made on the earthworks, and were readily repulsed, as the short range enabled the battery to inflict heavy damages on the attacking parties. During an all night attack, the enemy got in the works for a moment, but was driven out quickly by Texas troops, musket butts and frying pans being skilfully handled in the medley, and the fourth gun, under corporal E. G. Steane, enfiladed the over-climb-

ers. A good deal of wild firing was done by the enemy's artillery during the several days passed here; their wildest projectiles ranged considerably above the earthworks and fell with loud thud and shower of dust in the ravine beyond. During the enormous racket on the 12th of May, when the "horse-shoe" loop was surprised and captured, firing was kept up by the enemy's artillery in front of the Howitzers' position. Perceiving, at nightfall, that all his efforts were fruitless, Grant, with an obstinacy not exhibited in the previous chiefs of his army, evacuated Spotsylvania C. H., and renewed his flanking towards Richmond. Many novel mementoes of the fight were gathered on the field by the Howitzers, who discovered that their fire had been very effective in strewing the field with blue coated corpses. General Lee decided to withdraw to Hanover Junction, and doubtless this was the only course open to him, for the two armies had grown quite

disproportionate, his own through continual depletions, the enemy's through continual reinforcements. At Hanover Junction desultory artillery shooting was merely engaged in, and, after a few days of marching, battle was joined at Cold Harbor, for the second time in its history. It was the last great battle on Virginia soil, and in fact the last of the war. The fighting was a repetition of that at Spotsylvania C. H., though of a sharper, more concentrated character. The enemy's sharpshooters had attained great accuracy, and the least object, a head or an arm, shown above the earthworks was almost with certainty hit by them. The battery, also here placed behind a protective line and exposed to close range return fire, was hotly engaged, and lost its captain, Edward S. McCarthy, who was instantly killed during the action, on the 3rd of June. Lieutenant R. M. Anderson, succeeded to the command, by promotion, and remained captain to the end of the war.

CHAPTER XXII.

AFTER the battle at Cold Harbor, Grant, in continuing his flank movements, swung his army across the James to Petersburg, and the Howitzers took position on the line of earthworks extending from the river to that town, and about eight miles from the latter. Their camp, on Dunn's Farm, was permanent for the season and during the remainder of the siege of Richmond. Their military duties were confined to maintaining a state of expectancy and readiness; their active operations were quite suspended, for pitched battles were over. The camp was made comfortable, and, later on, winter quarters were as lively and agreeable as usual. The facilities for visiting Richmond by train, foot or horse, had never been so great, and furloughs and leaves were liberally granted.

During the course of the discouraging winter, when the Confederacy seemed to be visibly falling to pieces, every device was put in practice "to kill time." Improvised amusements were the order of day and night. There were many amusing occurrences, and many practical jokes were played on the innocent. For instance, during a cold spell of weather some of the more frolicsome veterans managed to pass off instructions on the novices of the night guard "to blow in the vents of the cannon in order to keep them clear," which operation brought forth a full budget of experiences and gossip for the next day. Many were the "boxes" and other good things that the company received, from their families in Richmond, by the railroad which passed through the camp-grounds and was handy in bringing over relatives and friends to "see the boys." So the winter wore away, the number of defenders constantly diminishing, men and horses growing thinner, the lines sparsely occupied,

provisions and forage reduced. At last, on the 1st of April, the crisis was reached. Grant saw his chance to open the spring campaign early, and pushed forward to the assault, which could not be resisted. After a light engagement, General Lee hastily retreated, with what force and material he could muster together, and many guns had to be left behind, because horses, either starved or killed off, were lacking to drag them away. The Howitzers had preserved their own horses. Then commenced the retreat, which lasted up to the final place of surrender at Appomattox C. H. The battery had its full share in this week's campaign of steady hardship, privation and skirmishing. The sharp combat of Sailor's Creek showed conclusively that both advance and retreat were cut off for the noble remnant of the Army of Northern Virginia, and, having done all that could be done, General Lee surrendered. In sorrow and anguish came the abrupt closing of the strug-

gle for the great principle of self-government founded and developed in Virginia. In the sadness and vexation of these last moments, the guns of the Howitzer battery were formally buried, laid away from all sight under the ground; they no longer belonged to Virginia, but they had done her good service, just as the dead and the living of the whole army had done her good service. Materially viewed, all was lost. In reality Virginia had triumphed. Her cause was won—a fact then instinctively felt, though obscured, since placed in clear light. Her victory was a moral one, costly, but enduring—to yield fruit. It is only by right derived from this struggle, from this moral victory, that Virginia, in union with the fast developing South, now stands loftily erect, respected and honored everywhere, utterly untouched by the workings of the malicious or the utterances of the foolish.

CHAPTER XXIII.

CAMPAIGNING, throughout, was much enlivened by a lavish flow of humor from "the professionals," who were never at a loss to turn anything to use. They were always at hand, and, even if they could have left the company, they relished its applause too keenly to have done so. Their inventions, anecdotes, remodeled stories, and gossip yielded endless entertainment. The originality of "these set sort of" Howitzers was unmistakable, their naturalness genuine, and, whether in camp or on the road, their flashes lit up a general merriment. There were many of these conspicuous characters, "originals," after various patterns, found during the four years in a company of such exceptionally good material. Witty commanders like "John," "Tom," "Ben," "Monkey," not to mention the long list,

were invincible in their respective veins, irrepressible in spirits, and indispensable to the general well being. Their observant powers had a fine field to work in. They made profuse use of nicknames, and the brands they stamped were indelible, far from being forgotten after this long lapse of time. A mere enumeration of some of them is sufficient to instantly and vividly recall to any veteran's mind heaps upon heaps of souvenirs, words, places, faces. Here are a few photographs:—"Suggs," "Prindle," "Monkey," "Sandusky," "Joe Miller," "Pinetop," "Beau," "The Baron," "Tantrobobus," "The Brigand," "Old Mortality," "Skipper," "Lucas," "Roger."

The company was kept well recruited, generally with those corresponding to the original members. The dates of arrival of some of the more distinguished recruits, who became "pillars" in the organization, were referred to as the events in its life. Transfers from other companies

were abundantly made to its ranks, not from them, except by way of promotion, and of this latter category there was quite a number. To be a member was really better than being a commissioned officer outside, or, indeed, inside the company, so cherished and pleasant was it. There was no ambition displayed by any of the privates to hold any office, from captaincy to corporalship; discipline did not pinch and all were equally a band of brothers fighting for Virginia. Offices, at elections, went as it were by default, almost to any one, to those who would take them rather than to seekers, because of these there were none to speak of. However, "public opinion" saw that only the fit should hold command.

CHAPTER XXIV.

THE battery suffered severely in the great battles fought by the Army of Northern Virginia, in all of which except two, Cedar Run and Second Manassas, it shared. Some of its best members perished on the battle-field. In killed and wounded, in deaths from wounds and illness, many were cut off in the very flower of their youth. Captain Edward S. McCarthy was killed on the field of second Cold Harbor, after having held the chief command of the battery over two years. He was instantly killed by a sharpshooter's ball which penetrated the middle of his forehead just as he arose from behind the earthwork to inspect the enemy's position. By the death of this gallant officer, the company lost not only an able, efficient head, but a personal friend, as he was

to all its members. His judicious course in camp and on the field was fully appreciated, and his generous, high spirit endeared him to every one under his orders. John Herring and W. L. Waddill were killed at Malvern Hill. Morrison, while acting as driver, was killed at the battle of Sharpsburg, by the explosion, just over his head, of a shell which cut him half in two. Nat. Selden and Tom Barksdale were killed at Chancellorsville, the first so young in years and appearance as to have been called a "thirteen-year old boy," by his joking comrades. Allen Morton and Dewees Ogden were killed in action during the battle of Gettysburg. Allen Morton was gunner of the first piece, and when in the act of performing his duty as such, steadily sighting and directing the gun, was torn into fragments by a shell which exploded where he was standing. Ogden, while the battery was firing as rapidly as possible, ran up to his gun with a shell for use and was felled dead to

the ground by a shrapnell shot. Henry Terrell was also killed at Gettysburg, but lingered a short while in the field hospital after having been struck. Cary Eggleston was mortally wounded at the battle of Spotsylvania C. H., wherein he displayed a reckless bravery, and, when being borne off the field, enthusiastically shouted in response to the inquiry of a general "Who have you got there?"— "Only another school teacher in the Confederacy, General!" Amputation of his arm resulted in his death at the field hospital. John Moseley was killed at Cold Harbor by a sharpshooter's shot which struck him squarely in the forehead. Charles Croxton, after being promoted to a lieutenancy in a cavalry regiment, was killed in the battles around Richmond. George E. King, who started out with the company as its twelve year old English drummer boy, joined another command, after the first battle, and later was killed. In the early days of the war, get-

ting rid of the inactivity of camp life was frequently secured through volunteering for action in the numerous skirmishes that took place. During a skirmish in which the battery was engaged on the Potomac in August, 1861, John Barr volunteered, after his section had ceased firing, to go with Captain Ball's cavalry troop for the purpose of further annoying the enemy before the fight should cease, and in so doing became the first wounded Howitzer. Tom Whiting was severely wounded in the battle of Williamsburg and incapacitated for further service in the field. George R. Crump was severely wounded in the battle of Seven Pines, incapacitated for further service, and obliged to leave the army. Charles E. Wingo was wounded in the arm and leg at the battle of Sharpsburg so as to unfit him for further duty with the army. When his arm was shattered by the projectile, he hastily left the gun to reach the shade of a tree some little distance away, and, as he had

fastened to his side the pouch of friction primers, the gunner, Charles L. Todd, knowing that the gun was useless without primers, ran after him, and Lieutenant Anderson, seeing both speeding off, ran shouting after them, whereupon the general commanding the supporting brigade also sent a colonel running after all three to see what was the matter, which, however, ended satisfactorily, without more ado. Such an occurrence was comical, but there was also danger in it, for panics on battle-fields are recorded that were due to a less disturbing accident. John B. Royall was wounded in the battle of Chancellorsville, disabled for active duty, detailed to the signal service, and was instantly killed by a shell from a gunboat which fired on the blockade runner he served upon near the harbor of Wilmington. David S. Doggett, after joining White's Battalion of Virginia cavalry, lost his right arm during one of the largest cavalry engage-

ments of the war at Brandy Station, on June 9, 1863, between Stuart and Pleasanton. William P. Smith lost his leg in the battle of Gettysburg, having been struck by a shell that necessitated amputation, and he was left a prisoner on the field, but soon returned to Virginia. P. McNamee also lost his leg in the battle of Gettysburg, and was left a prisoner in the hospital on that field. Ben Lambert's right arm was shattered at second Cold Harbor, and, by a singular coincidence, on the anniversary of the same day, and at the same hour, that the same arm had been previously wounded during the notorious "Kansas War"; he was permanently disabled while acting as number one at the fourth gun. Charles M. Pleasants was struck in the leg on the field of Spotsylvania C. H. and disabled for furthur service. Among other wounded, those who received slight or flesh wounds, were R. A. Stiles, Bob McCandlish, Henry Kep-

pler, Charles Poindexter, Ned Snead, John Pleasants, John A. Scott, James T. Gray, John B. Wise, Harry Sublett.

The company was compelled to leave several of its members behind on the field of Gettysburg, and they became prisoners; like the other prisoners in northern camps and forts, they were treated as badly as was to be expected under the circumstances. These captured Howitzers were: James T. Gray, Charles Poindexter, Henry Keppler, William P. Smith, P. McNamee, Henry Barnes, Wallace Washington—all either wounded or ill and required by the surgeons to remain behind in the field hospital. After the first battle of Manassas, the company was joined by many eager young men, some of them boys in point of years, for whom school or business had no attractions equal to those of the tented field. Just about this time, the camp at Centreville had the pleasure of making the acquaintance of T. D. Moncure and of welcoming him as a member in the ranks;

it was not long before he became a universal favorite and so remained to the end, closing as a lieutenant of the company. A few weeks later, at Leesburg, James T. Gray came up from Richmond to join "the Howitzers." He was a mere boy, fresh from Randolph Macon college, on vacation, who had, after much pleading with his father, obtained consent to join the army, wherein his elder brother was already serving. In his youthful inexperience he stipulated with the captain that he should not be made a driver, or given a pair of horses to take care of, but be allotted an apparently more exalted position at the gun. He remarked to the captain that he knew nothing about taking care of horses, which confession was verified subsequently when the inexorable necessities of "detailing" put him to the task of currying a team; his practice was to curry both horses at once, and the result of this was merely to furnish more matter for rippling laughter to the irrepressible

"Lieutenant Nimmo," mostly "John," or "Old John," who, like a good wit, made use of anything. While the battery was in camp near Orange C. H. on one occasion, "Jimmy" became "chief surgeon" of the "Doctors' Squad," a well known burlesque organization got up expressly for the purpose of looking after the health of the four detachments, in ways and with prescriptions that were peculiar, though certainly not bland. After the battle of Chancellorsville, he fell ill and was sent to the receiving hospital at Richmond, but, as the army soon started for Pennsylvania, he managed to escape without a discharge and joined the march in the Valley; though his illness barely enabled him to keep up, he worked at his gun in the battle of Gettysburg, and, at its ending, his ailing condition was such that the doctors ordered him to be left behind in the field hospital. After passing fifteen months in prison, he was discharged, rejoined the Howitzers, and served till the end.

A few nights preceding the surrender at Appomattox C. H., while engaged cooking with his mess of the fourth detachment, a musket ball fired by the enemy struck him in the breast, but, as it was spent, it could not penetrate the rolled blanket and coat around his body, and merely left a stunning, bad bruise. Next morning, on perceiving a big black spot on his breast, he remarked to a companion: "Ned, mortification has set in!" "Yes, I reckon it has, Jimmy," was "The Baron's" laughing answer. "The Baron" had his own way of laughing occasionally, though generally so grave, solemn and precise in his natural style, as to have suggested this title at the hands of one of his best friends. On one occasion, when standing around a camp fire, he remarked in a deep, bass voice, and way-off look up at the tops of the trees, to a party just up from Richmond, "Anything on the boar-rds to-day?" One of his tent mates indistinctly making out this reference to the newspaper

bulletin boards immediately called out: "What's that you say, Ned?" "The Baron," with a withering glance: "I didn't speak to you, sir!" "Well, I noticed you were not around to-day when we pitched the tent!" was the snubbed tent mate's parting shot. This sort of joking was invariably seasoned with the nicest of amenities, by way of contrast to the rude doings of warfare.

CHAPTER XXV.

An association of veterans, or of those who belonged to the Howitzers' organizations during the war, gives an annual banquet on the 13th of December, anniversary of the battle of Fredericksburg, and it furnishes the opportunity for pleasant reunion and agreeable recollections. These banquets are attended by the new, or present, company of Howitzers, which cherishes the reputation that the original company won in the field, and keeps its flag flying. During the recent trip of the Howitzers to New Orleans, for the purpose of taking part in the Mardi Gras festivities, some of the veterans went along and tramped about the streets there in good military style; special honors were paid them by the Washington Artillery which had in the olden time been so well received in Richmond,

and which won such a high reputation on Virginia's fields. Naturally all veterans take pleasure in relating and hearing of campaign experiences. The Howitzer veterans do not deny themselves this pleasure. Wherever they may be, in whatever land or clime, where one or two, or more, meet, there the copious military past is dived into, the subject of their army life is brought up for delightful mention and discussion, and they are momentarily carried back to the days of their youth and the stirring period of ever memorable events. "Age cannot wither, nor custom stale" the infinite variety of these recollections.

The generation stepping upon the scene since the war has unquestionably heard much of this theme, perhaps an excess that has at times interfered with their own present doings, and given birth to a sensation of monotonousness creeping over them and enfolding them like a fog, seen through darkly; doubtless so, and such sensation is naturally ex-

cusable, for people must live in the present, and "things that move sooner catch the eye than what not stirs." It has been said that more "war talk" goes on in Virginia than anywhere else. Yes, and for cause. Its memories and results are not of the fading kind: verbal narrations by the participators over, the topic will still stand on the page of history, and it will stand there firm.

A truth, a great fact, being imperishable, lives of itself. Its life is so solid that it needs no support, going on its way unconsciously or only self-consciously, and so there is no requirement for it as it imposes itself. When people get up in the morning, they do not take note of the fact that they are possessed of a pair of hands, but simply use them. The struggle of 1861-65 is an illustration of such a kind of life. It asks no favors, begs no notice or "honorable mention," because it is indelibly impressed, not merely on the page of history, but on the stock of people who own these

fifteen Southern states. In other words, it is a constituent part of them, entering into the warp and woof of their very being. Superficial utterances on the part of the thoughtless and the ignorant are of course natural, and continuous, but without any consequence. What gives weight to Virginia and the South to-day?—what has caused their astonishing recuperation, their relative prosperity, and substantial position before the world? The performance of duty, of having been true to themselves at a critical juncture. The high characteristics inherited from the master race of the globe enabled them first to start on a high plane, and then to keep there when a redoubtable effort was made to shove them off, and there they stand now, even on a still higher one: Smith and Washington at one end, Lee and Jackson at the other. Are the sons and daughters different from the fathers and mothers? Not so—they are the same, and must remain so, for their nature can not

change. Yes, present and future generations would doubtless do as well, may be even better, under emergencies, whether these should be of the same sort as those that accidentally cropped out in 1861, or otherwise. Meanwhile it is by no means amiss that earnest attention in present affairs, or as commonly remarked "a wrapping up in business and money making," should be exhibited in the South, or that comforts and improvements should be sought after. All the better—it is commendable that they should be. Has not the parent country, England, followed such a course, does she not give such an example at the present moment, and yet has not her history proved that she never failed herself, and is there not an absolute conviction everywhere that she would act dutifully to and for herself upon any pinch whatever? Both artificial and natural history prove that the elements directing a strong race of people are compulsory, irresistibly vital and

enduring. "No history on our side!" Yes, the very best—a living one. What was the war? The upholding of the principle of self-government, involving truth, justice, fair play, under a system of proper checks and disciplines, divine and human, the same principle that has long, virtually, underlaid England, that underlies the South, and could also have underlaid the Puritan stock of the North if it had not been so greedy, fanatical, unprincipled, and foolishly opened the doors of its section to flooding by continental Europeans. Now, that these, after being used to kill the soldiers of the South, have crowded North and West, the rate being two foreigners to one native on the grand total of population, the Puritan descendants begin to feel where the shoe is pinching in their vast Bedlam of discordant races speaking outlandish tongues; but there is little or no prospect of relief for them, and, truly, another result of their folly and mischief even

squints plainly at the forming of separate clanships, or nationalities, within their own borders. Nemesis is in their homes, tramping about rather promiscuously, in various ways, financial, political, moral, social and especially anarchistic. It may be a penance imposed that they should now be opening their eyes to the truth that local rights, state rights, individual rights, do contain some grains of man's highest civilization, and that only those who deserve and maintain them are allowed the high privilege of indulging in them. The meaning of the war, all around, looms up in so much clearer light. Secession was "magnificent," unparalleled as a contention for high principle, though perhaps strict martinets may claim that the war itself was not scientific militarism, and hence horribly mismanaged. They may possibly be right, but their claim would signify nothing in face of its infinitely higher predominant aim of supporting Constitutional Right, altogether in which

assertive spirit we now see that it was conducted, and, in the nature of things, only could have been conducted. The Southern leaders, civil and military, corresponded to their people:—neither could be wrenched from settled moorings, from trained and inherited practices, in order to secure unity of military direction—the prerequisite of dictatorship to yield the fruit of conquest.

CHAPTER XXVI.

The following are the names of all who were members of the company from April 21st, 1861, to April 9th, 1865. (*Started out with.)

*ANDERSON, CAPT. R. M.,
ANDERSON, JAMES E.,
ANDERSON, JUNIUS H.,
*ANDERSON, LUCIUS,
ANDERSON, LEWIS,
*ANDERSON, THOS. B.,
ARENTS, FRANK,
*ARMISTEAD, LIEUT. R.,
*ARMISTEAD. THOS. S.,
ADKISSON, JOSEPH,
*AUGUST, JAMES A.,
AYRES, SAMUEL,
AYRES, JOHN,
AYRES, THOS.,
*BARNES, EDWARD,
*BARNES, FRANK,
*BARNES, HENRY,

Carter, Dr. L. W.,
Carter, Samuel,
Carter, James,
Cary, William,
Cary, Pike,
Camm, Charles,
Crouch, Prof. F. N.,
*Cullingworth, J. N.,
*Cooke, John Esten,
Coyle, T. R.,
Cubbage, W.,
Close, Robert,
*Crump, George R.,
*Croxton, Charles,
Chesterman, A. D.,
*Dibrell, Anthony,
Dibrell, Watson S.,
Dame, W. M.,
*Daniel, Fred. S.,
*Davis, D. O.,
*Drewry, W. S.,
Denny, J.,
Denman, A. M.,
Dupuy, B. H.,
*Doggett, D. S.,
Drewry, T.,
Davis, Joe,

*Early, George W.,
*Eggleston, J. Cary,
Edmundson, Henry,
*Ellett, James M.,
Ellyson, W. P.,
Eustace, Wm.,
Exall, George,
Ellis, George H.,
Friend, Charles,
Finney, W.,
*Flournoy, John,
French, J.,
*Gibson, James W.,
Gray, James T.,
Gray, Edward,
Gray, Somerville,
Gray, Charles,
Guigon, Alexander B.,
Grundy, T. B.,
Grigg, George L.,
*Goddin, E. C.,
*Gretter, W. P.,
Harrison, Walter J.,
Harrison, Henry,
Harrison, George B.,
*Harrington, Charles A.,
*Huffard, D. S.,

Hardy, William J.,
*Harvey, W. L.,
*Harvey, Martin L.,
*Howard, Charles W.,
Harwood, Charles,
*Harris, B. F.,
Higgerson, A.,
Howard, John,
*Herring, John,
Herring, Eldridge,
Herring, William,
Kean, W. C.,
*Kean, W. C. Jr.,
*Keppler, Addison,
Keppler, Henry,
Kinsolving, C. J.,
*Knight, R. D.,
Keiser, C.,
Kelly, Robert,
Lambert, J. Ben.,
Lamkin, William,
Lee, George,
*Lewis, W. T.
*Lewis, C. Montgomery,
*Leake, P. S.,
McNamee, J.,
*McCarthy, Capt. E. S.,

*McCarthy, Lieut. D. S.,
*McCreery, J. V. L.,
*McCabe, James, E.,
McCandlish, Robert,
McKenna, John,
McMillan, Charles,
McReynolds, S.,
*Macon, Thomas J.,
*Marsden, Robert,
Marsh, Henry,
Maury, Robert H. Jr.,
Minor, J. B.,
Moore, W. S.,
Moore, R. F.,
Moore, Edward,
Martin, S. Taylor,
*Meade, Hodijah L.,
*Moseley, John,
*Massie, Henry,
Maloney, P.,
Moran, Milton,
*Michaud, Paul,
*Morton, Allen,
Morrison, Charles,
Moncure, Lieut. T. D.,
*Nimmo, Lieut. John,
Niven, R. M.,

Ogden, Dewees,
*Palmer, Capt. W. P.,
*Palmer, William,
Peachy, Griffin,
Perry, W. H.,
*Pleasants, Charles M.,
Pleasants, W. H.,
*Pleasants, John,
*Poindexter, George H.,
Poindexter, Charles,
Page, William,
Page, Carter,
Page, John,
Pollard, Byrd,
Price, Overton B.,
*Powell, Junius L.,
*Powell, Hugh L.,
Parrott, A. B.,
*Puryear, W. H.,
*Rahm, Frank,
Rahm, Adolphus,
Read, N. C.,
Read, Lewis,
*Richardson, R. E.,
Richardson, George,
Richardson, Abner,
Robinson, Leigh,

ROYALL, JOHN B.,
ROYALL, R. W.,
*SHIELDS, CAPT. J. C.,
*STEANE, EDMUND G.,
STILES, R. A.,
STILES, ROBERT,
STILES, EUGENE,
*SUBLETT, HENRY,
SCOTT, JOHN A.,
SCOTT, CHARLES,
SELDEN, NATHANIEL,
*SELDEN, CHARLES,
SNEAD, J. H.,
SNEAD, E. B.,
*SCLATER, L. H.,
*SIMPSON, J. H.,
SMITH, W. P.,
SMITH, BATHURST,
SEARS, DE WITT,
SIMONS, W. T.,
*SCHOOLER, JOHN H.,
SEAY, JOSEPH,
SKINNER, ED.,
*TOWNSEND, H. C.,
*TATUM, W. H.,
TATUM, JOHN C.,
*TODD, CHARLES L.,

*Todd, William R.,
*Taliaferro, Whit.,
Todd, John,
Tucker, Ben.,
*Trabue, C. E.,
Tyler, J. H.,
Terrell, Henry,
Vaiden, Sam.,
Vest, George,
*Williams, Lieut. Henry S.,
Williams, J. Peter,
Williams, Watson,
Williams, Frank S.,
Williams, Fred.,
*Wyatt, John W.,
*Wyatt, Richard W.,
Wyatt, Thomas,
*Wayt, William,
Wise, Lewis,
*Wise, John B.,
Washington, Wallace,
Wingo, Charles E.,
*Wortham, R. C.,
*Whiting, Thomas,
*Waddill, W. L.,
White, William,
Wharton, R. G.,
Wynne, Arthur,
Wood, John P.,

5883H

www.ingramcontent.com/pod-product-compliance
Lightning Source LLC
Chambersburg PA
CBHW031906220426
43663CB00006B/797